John's Financial Funnies," your ultimate guide to navigating the world of finances with a dose of humor

I0408656

CHAPTER 1: BROKE AND HILARIOUS BEGINNINGS

Dive into your own financial mishaps and laugh-worthy money blunders, proving that we've all been there.

CHAPTER 2: THE ART OF BUDGETING WITHOUT LOSING YOUR SANITY

Teach budgeting basics with a twist—using rap metaphors and hilarious analogies to make money management more relatable.

CHAPTER 3: THE DOS AND DON'TS OF DEALING WITH DEBT DRAMA

Share strategies for tackling debt while cracking jokes about the absurdity of some financial situations.

CHAPTER 4: INVESTMENTS UNLEASHED—FROM STOCKS TO SNEAKERS

Break down investment concepts with quirky comparisons, like treating stocks like collecting rare sneakers.

CHAPTER 5: SIDE HUSTLES FOR HUSTLERS

Explore creative side hustle ideas, ranking them based on the number of laughs they generate.

CHAPTER 6: CONQUERING THE CREDIT CARD CONUNDRUM

Explain credit cards, credit scores, and the importance of responsible use through humorous anecdotes.

CHAPTER 7: RETIREMENT PLANNING FOR ETERNAL RAPPERS

Guide readers through retirement planning with references to the hip-hop legends who are still making bank.

CHAPTER 8: CRUSHING YOUR FINANCIAL FEARS WITH COMEDY

Address common financial fears and worries using humor to highlight the exaggerations we often make.

CHAPTER 9: LOVE AND MONEY—A STAND-UP ROMANCE

Blend relationship advice with finance, using funny stories to show how money can make or break love.

CHAPTER 10: LAUGHING ALL THE WAY TO THE BANK

End on a high note by sharing success stories of readers who turned their financial situations around while having a good laugh.

CHAPTER 1: BROKE AND HILARIOUS BEGINNINGS

venture together.Ah, the battle of those early days when your ledger felt as vacant as a show scene during a Monday evening. We've all been there, old buddy, counting the loose coins like it's an expedition and living off cup noodles like they're haute cooking. But, hey, we should go for a walk through a world of fond memories and think back about those broke and very funny starting points.

The Dumpster Jumping Quandary: A Mission for Food

At any point wound up looking into a dumpster, contemplating the probability of scoring a few somewhat swollen however possibly still consumable bananas? That's right, we've all been that courageous hero on a mission for food. Who realize that moderation could prompt such trying ventures? But, hey, those bananas were likely the most thrilling thing to happen to you that week, and they sure made for a few extraordinary stories.

Do-It-Yourself Feasting: When Your Culinary Abilities Hit Absolute bottom

Recollect whenever you first endeavored to prepare a dinner that didn't include emptying milk into grain? We should simply say that your endeavors at connoisseur cooking looked like a greater amount of a vanguard craftsmanship project than a banquet fit for sovereignty. Yet, hello, those microwave culinary examinations were joined by a heavy portion of chuckling and an illustration in embracing your inward culinary craftsman.

Couponing Narratives: An Adventure of Saving (or Attempting to)

Ok, the delights of couponing — a game that joins technique, math, and the excitement of saving a couple of bucks. However, we should be genuine, the vast majority of us have gazed at a heap of terminated coupons with a similar disarray as unraveling old symbolic representations. Your undertakings in the realm of couponing most likely elaborate fearless efforts to dominate the artistic work of "coupon stacking," regardless of whether it brought about the checkout line likeness a satire show.

The Incomparable Garments Trade: Style on a Careful Financial plan

Who needs a glitzy shopping binge when you can have a closet "trade party"? You've probably exchanged pants that fit like thin shorts for shirts that could twofold as dresses. What's more, I could go on and on about the amazing sock-manikin theater you arranged when the socks strangely vanished individually.

Eventually, these cleverly broke starting points are the stuff of legends, the accounts that bond companions over chuckling and the information that making due on ramen assembles character (and maybe some sodium-related wellbeing concerns). Thus, we should raise a virtual toast to those times when your wallet was lighter, however your heart was certainly more full with stories of monetary experiences that molded you into the wise cash maestro you are today.

CHAPTER 2: THE ART OF BUDGETING WITHOUT LOSING YOUR SANITY

Planning — a word that can either make your eyes stare off into the great unknown or creep you out. In any case, dread not, old buddy, since we're going to transform planning into a show-stopper of monetary artfulness, all while safeguarding your mental soundness. Prepare to learn "The Craft of Planning Without Losing Your Mental stability."

Planning 101: The Material of Your Monetary Magnum opus

Consider your financial plan a material anticipating your inventive touch. There's really no need to focus on tightening yourself; about creating an arrangement assists you with accomplishing your objectives while considering a touch of monetary space to breathe. Envision you're forming a rap stanza — every dollar has its place, and each cost adds to the orchestra of your monetary excursion.

The Hip-Bounce Hustle: Dispensing Assets Like a Genius

Very much like a rap tune has various components that meet up amicably, your spending plan has classifications that need their time at the center of attention. Food, lease, utilities — these are your sections. Reserve funds, speculations, and fun cash — those are your snappy tunes. Balance is the beat that keeps the melody streaming without a hitch.

The Free-form Flex: Embracing Startling Turns

Life loves tossing curves, and your financial plan should be pretty much as adaptable as your stream. Leave space for extemporization, as you do when freestyling on the mic. Startling costs? No perspiration, you have a backup stash for that. Furthermore, recollect, similarly as the best rappers adjust to any beat, you also can change your spending plan to deal with anything life tosses your direction.

Planning Beats: Transforming Saving into a Game

Planning doesn't need to be a drag. Consider it a game where you're the DJ, blending and remixing your monetary tracks. Set achievements and celebrate hitting them, very much like dropping the ideal rhyme in your rap. Furthermore, hello, on the off chance that you save more than anticipated, indulge yourself with a little prize — you deserve it!

The Reprise Impact: Surveying and Refining

Very much like you tweak rap verses prior to delivering a track, your financial plan needs occasional updates. Investigate your spending designs, change your distributions, and put forth new objectives. Keep in mind, a spending plan is a living report that develops as you do, guaranteeing you're generally on the way to monetary fame.

Thus, my planning virtuoso, embrace the craft of planning like you would another beat. There's really no need to focus on probation; it's about strengthening. With a very much created spending plan, you're assuming command over your monetary predetermination while watching out for your funny bone. All things considered, a decent spending plan is a definitive rap fight against overspending and monetary turmoil.

CHAPTER 3: THE DOS AND DON'TS OF DEALING WITH DEBT DRAMA

Ok, obligation — the busybody of the monetary world. Yet, dread not, since we're going to spread out a definitive playbook for taking care of obligation with the artfulness of a rap whiz. Prepare to learn "The Customs of Managing Obligation Show."

Do: Stand up to Obligation Head-On, Similar to a Fight Rap

You know how in a rap fight, you deal with your rival directly? Indeed, obligation is your rival, and evasion isn't a choice. Accumulate every one of your obligations, spread them out like a melodious test, and face them with a decided demeanor. Similarly as a rapper concentrates on their opponent's shortcomings, concentrate on your obligations and make a game plan.

Don't: Disregarding Obligation Won't Cause It To vanish

Overlooking obligation resembles disregarding a terrible rhyme in your verses — it will not mystically vanish. It'll probably develop and turn into a much greater obstacle, as a matter of fact. Rather than imagining it doesn't exist, stand up to it like you would an extreme section: with mental fortitude and an eagerness to get to the next level.

Do: Set Up a Reimbursement Technique, Otherwise known as Your Monetary Remix

Each great melody needs a remix, and your obligation reimbursement procedure is the same. Separate your obligations into reasonable parcels, and tackle them individually. Similarly as you'd create an incredible section, create a technique that spotlights on taking care of exorbitant interest obligations first, while making least installments on others.

Don't: Depending Exclusively on Least Installments

Paying just the base on your obligations resembles recording a track however never delivering it — you're passing up the chance for significant effect. Least installments keep you in the know yet don't assist you with getting away from the obligation cycle. Take a stab at more than the base to pick up speed and pay off your obligations quicker.

Do: Assemble a Just-in-case account Like You're Building Your Rhyme Arms stockpile

Similarly as a rapper's stockpile of rhymes is their wellbeing net during a fight, your backup stash is your security net even with startling monetary difficulties. Having a couple of months of costs buried gives you true serenity, very much like having a debilitated section prepared to drop immediately.

Try not to: Resort to Handy solution Arrangements

Utilizing one obligation to pay off another is like utilizing a powerless zinger to save a rhyme — it could get you out of a difficult situation briefly, yet it's anything but a maintainable arrangement. Stay away from convenient solution strategies that could deteriorate what is happening over the long haul.

Do: Look for Help When the Refrain Gets Extreme

In the rap world, even the best specialists team up for the ideal track. Also, when obligation feels difficult, make sure to exhortation from monetary specialists or credit advisors. They can assist you with making a strategy that will make them tackle obligation like a melodious virtuoso.

Try not to: Let Obligation Characterize Your Personality

Similarly as you're not characterized by a solitary rap, you're not characterized by your obligation. It's a test you're handling, not an impression of what your identity is. Remain positive and watch out for your comical inclination — you're on the way to conquering obligation show and getting a more splendid monetary future.

Thus, we should deal with obligation like a beat that requirements dominating. By following these dos and keeping away from the don'ts, you'll change obligation show into an account of win, similar as transforming an abnormal rhyme into a strong refrain. You have this!

CHAPTER 4: INVESTMENTS UNLEASHED—FROM STOCKS TO SNEAKERS

Okay, now is the ideal time to plunge into the universe of speculations — a domain where your monetary gifts can sparkle as brilliantly as your rhymes on an exceptional track. Prepare to find out about "Ventures Released," where we'll investigate everything from conventional stocks to the startling appeal of speculation grade tennis shoes.

Stocks: The Beat of the Venture World

Consider stocks the cadence segment of your monetary portfolio. Very much like in a rap tune, where each instrument adds to the general song, stocks are one of the key parts driving your venture process. Research organizations, businesses, and patterns like you would investigate melodic impacts for your next show-stopper.

Bonds: The Smooth Progression of Consistent Returns

Bonds resemble the smooth, melodic sections that add equilibrium to a rap track. They offer more unsurprising returns contrasted with stocks, giving dependability to your portfolio's cadence. Similarly as your verses recount a story, bonds recount the tale of a consistent revenue stream over the long run.

Land: Putting resources into Substantial Beats

Putting resources into land is like making a multifaceted rap track with various components meeting up for a unique sound. Land properties give substantial resources that can see the value in esteem over the long run. Whether it's private, business, or even a computerized property in a virtual world, land speculations add profundity to your monetary sythesis.

Cryptographic money: The Offbeat Refrain

Cryptographic money is the trump card refrain in your venture melody. Very much like a remarkable rhyme plan can separate your track, cryptographic forms of money offer a new, computerized method for effective money management. Examination and mindfulness are vital, as the cryptographic money market can be essentially as erratic as a free-form fight.

Elective Speculations: The Remix of Broadening

Broadening resembles remixing your speculations — it mixes it up and flavor to your portfolio. Elective speculations, like valuable metals, collectibles, and indeed, even venture grade tennis shoes, can be a great method for enhancing. Similarly as you try different things with new sounds in your rap, consider investigating elective speculations with a blend of interest and wariness.

The Beat of Tolerance: Long haul versus Present moment

Effective money management, such as making a rap, requires both momentary explosions of innovativeness and long haul commitment. A few ventures might yield speedy outcomes, similar to a snappy tune that sticks in your mind. Others require tolerance, such as fostering your expressive abilities over the long haul. Offsetting momentary successes with long haul development is the cadence that makes your speculation portfolio amicable.

The Remix: Rebalancing and Investigating

Recall how you remix your tracks to keep them new and applicable? Your venture portfolio needs a remix as well. Consistently audit and rebalance your speculations to guarantee they line up with your monetary objectives. As the market and your life develop, change your blend to remain in line with your yearnings.

Thus, consider your venture process like creating a diagram besting collection. Every venture is a track, and your monetary portfolio is the collection all in all. With information, technique, and some of your brand name humor, you can make a speculation work of art that reverberates long into the future.

CHAPTER 5: SIDE HUSTLES FOR HUSTLERS

Aight, we should discuss second jobs — the gigs that supplement your primary hustle like a very much coordinated off the cuff in a rap stanza. In this section, we're plunging into "Part time jobs for Tricksters," where we'll investigate imaginative ways of enhancing your pay while keeping that hawker's soul alive.

Outsourcing: Rapping Your Abilities for Money

Similarly as you mesh words into verses, outsourcing permits you to mesh your abilities into rewarding tasks. Whether it's composition, visual depiction, coding, or counseling, your gifts can procure you a chunk of change as an afterthought. Consider outsourcing as your opportunity to drop visitor stanzas on another person's track.

Internet Selling: Transforming Mess into Cash

Recall that old mic you supplanted with a superior one? Or on the other hand those shoes that at this point not fit your style? Web based selling stages are your stage for transforming mess into difficult money. It's like teaming up with individual specialists — aside from your colleagues are individual purchasers and dealers in the computerized commercial center.

Mentoring and Instructing: Spreading Your Insight

Similarly as you've leveled up your rap abilities throughout the long term, you've probably turned into a specialist in different fields. Why not share that information? Offer mentoring, instructing, or even internet based courses to anxious students. It resembles training somebody to dominate an intricate rhyme conspire — they're gaining from the best.

Conveyance Driving: Bringing Beats and Burritos

Conveyance driving resembles conveying beats to the majority — you're carrying something significant to individuals' doorsteps. Whether it's food, bundles, or travelers, you're transforming your wheels into a wellspring of additional pay. Besides, it's an opportunity to investigate your city's areas like a genuine hip-bounce student of history.

Pet Sitting or Canine Strolling: Entertaining Four-Legged Fans

Pets resemble dedicated fans — they love you genuinely. Why not acquire from their love by offering pet sitting or canine strolling administrations? You'll get compensated to invest energy with shaggy companions, and they'll be your greatest team promoters.

Occasion DJ or MC: Facilitating a Melodic Get-together

You're as of now gifted at setting the temperament with your rap verses. What about doing likewise as an occasion DJ or MC? You'll be arranging melodic energies or advertising up the group, and getting compensated for it. It resembles facilitating a live exhibition with an alternate sort of mic in your grasp.

Leasing Your Space: Sharing Your Stage

On the off chance that you have additional room, leasing it out can be a goldmine. Whether it's an extra room, carport, or even your whole spot, stages like Airbnb let you capitalize on your space like it's a sold-out show setting.

Keep in mind: Equilibrium and Enthusiasm

Similarly as you balance your refrains and snares in a tune, you'll have to track down a side gig that supplements your fundamental gig without overpowering you. Pick something that lines up with your interests and gifts, so it seems more like a remunerating inventive pursuit than simply one more work.

In this way, how about we approach part time jobs like creating the ideal cooperation. Every one adds an interesting flavor to your monetary blend, transforming your hawker soul into an ensemble of chances. Whether it's conveying pizzas or conveying rap stanzas, each side gig is an opportunity to flex your abilities and lift your main concern.

CHAPTER 6: CONQUERING THE CREDIT CARD CONUNDRUM

Ok, Visas — a definitive situation with two sides in the monetary rap game. In any case, dread not, John, since we're going to separate the Mastercard problem like you analyze your rhymes. Prepare to find out about "Vanquishing the Visa Problem," where we'll explore the ups and downs of plastic cash with the artfulness of a rap maestro.

Grasping the Refrain: Visa Fundamentals

Consider your charge card as a melodious gadget — it can possibly lift your monetary exhibition or outing you up in the event that not utilized carefully. Comprehend the terms, loan costs, and credit limits. Similarly as you'd concentrate on your beat prior to freestyling, concentrate on your Mastercard expressions prior to swiping.

The Imbecile Lines: Mindful Mastercard Use

Mastercards resemble your lines in a rap — everything revolves around conveyance and timing. Utilize your charge card mindfully by covering the equilibrium every month. This forms a positive record as a consumer, very much like your smooth rhymes construct your standing.

The Snare: Building Credit Like a Hit Single

Similarly as a snappy snare makes a melody important, building credit is significant for your monetary standing. Standard and on-time installments are your snare, and a higher FICO rating is the graph besting hit you're holding back nothing. This opens ways to more readily loan costs and monetary open doors.

The Remix: Dealing with Various Cards

Dealing with various Visas resembles remixing an exemplary track — you want to keep up with equilibrium and congruity. On the off chance that you can oversee it, different cards can really upgrade your credit blend. In any case, similar to a perplexing beat, you really want to keep steady over installments and try not to get found out in a credit circle.

The Publicity: Rewards and Advantages

Visa rewards resemble the promotion libs that add energy to your rap. Cashback, travel focuses, or limits can be incredible advantages. Simply recall, the key is utilizing compensations for your potential benefit without overspending and falling into the obligation trap.

The Breakdown: Exorbitant Financing costs and Obligation

Exorbitant financing costs resemble a rapper's most obviously terrible pundits — they can destroy you if you don't watch out. Conveying an equilibrium on your charge card can prompt the obligation winding. Interest energizes heap like terrible surveys, making it harder to climb out.

The Free-form: Backup stash Over Credit

In a free-form rap, you adjust to the occasion. Likewise, for surprising costs, depend on your secret stash prior to going after your Visa. It resembles ad libbing a stanza on the spot as opposed to reusing old lines.

The Remix: Equilibrium Moves and Solidification

On the off chance that your Mastercard obligation feels like a disarranged track, consider a remix as equilibrium moves or combination credits. These procedures can assist you with dealing with your obligation by consolidating it into one reasonable installment.

The Great Finale: Shutting Unused Cards

Similarly as you refine your rap prior to delivering it, consider shutting unused Mastercards. Nonetheless, be careful — shutting cards can influence your financial assessment. It resembles resigning old tracks from your collection while as yet keeping your presentation strong.

Keep in mind: Your Credit Story

Very much like your rap process is extraordinarily yours, your record recounts your monetary story. Use Mastercards as instruments to construct a strong groundwork, not as a snare. With dependable use, you can dominate the Visa problem and make a monetary heritage that is basically as essential as your best stanzas.

Thus, move toward Visas like making a hit melody. Each swipe is a note in your monetary organization, and by excelling at mindful use, you're making a tune that will reverberate long into the future.

CHAPTER 7: RETIREMENT PLANNING FOR ETERNAL RAPPERS

Yo, People, we should discuss retirement arranging — a definitive beat drop in your monetary excursion. Be that as it may, just relax, retirement doesn't mean you're hanging up your mic. As a matter of fact, it's tied in with making way for a future where you can continue dropping those melodious jewels while residing serenely. Prepare to find out about "Retirement Making arrangements for Everlasting Rappers," where we'll set out the beat for getting your monetary future.

Setting the Stage: The Retirement Vision

Similarly as you plan the construction of your stanzas, imagine your retirement. What does it resemble? Might it be said that you are chilling on a tropical ocean side, hitting up open mics, or coaching youthful rappers? Characterize your retirement objectives, and let that vision guide your monetary choices.

The Benefits Refrain: Manager Supported Plans

Boss supported retirement plans resemble the stanzas in a tune — they give design to your monetary song. Boost commitments to plans like 401(k)s or 403(b)s to guarantee you're fabricating a strong starting point for retirement. Like creating serious areas of strength for a stanza establishes the vibe for the whole track.

Solo Vocation: Individual Retirement Records (IRAs)

Similarly as your performance profession adds a remarkable flavor to the rap game, Individual Retirement Records (IRAs) permit you to make your retirement work of art. Customary IRAs and Roth IRAs offer different duty benefits, so pick the one that reverberates with your monetary style.

The Remix: Enhance Your Ventures

Recall how you remix your tracks to keep them new? Expand your retirement speculations comparatively. Blend stocks, bonds, and different resources for make a balanced portfolio. Along these lines, you're prepared to drop some monetary insight no matter what the market's beat.

Keep the Stream: Customary Commitments

Similarly as you practice your stream to keep up with your rapping abilities, contribute routinely to your retirement accounts. Reliable commitments keep your retirement anticipate track, guaranteeing you're actually spitting bars even after the spotlight shifts.

The Element: Get up to speed Commitments

While you're highlighting on another person's track, you bring your A-game. Additionally, in the event that you're approaching retirement age and haven't saved however much you'd like, get up to speed commitments permit you to increase your reserve funds. It resembles dropping an unexpected refrain that captures everyone's attention.

Brilliant Years: Government managed retirement and Then some

Federal retirement aide resembles the heritage you abandon in your rap vocation — it's the finish of your persistent effort. While Government managed retirement gives a benchmark, make sure to consider other pay sources like ventures, benefits, and perhaps sovereignties from your unbelievable tracks.

The Reprise: Retirement Withdrawal Techniques

Your retirement is the fabulous finale of your monetary exhibition, and how you pull out reserves is your reprise. Set up a withdrawal technique that expands your assets while limiting charges. Similarly as you'd leave the crowd needing more with a reprise, ensure your retirement subsidizes last.

Keep in mind: Adaptability and Enthusiasm

Similarly as you adjust your stream to various beats, remain adaptable in your retirement plans. Life might toss startling rhythms your way, and having the adaptability to change your methodology is vital. What's more, similarly as your energy energizes your rap profession, let your enthusiasm guide your retirement interests. Keep those imaginative energies pumping in anything you decide to do.

In this way, , consider retirement arranging like delivering an awe-inspiring collection. Each monetary choice is a track that adds to your retirement orchestra. By setting the stage currently, you're guaranteeing that your future is as melodiously rich and agreeable as your most prominent hits.

CHAPTER 8: CRUSHING YOUR FINANCIAL FEARS WITH COMEDY

What up, G now is the ideal time to handle those monetary feelings of trepidation head-on, yet with a spot of humor that no one but you can give. In this section, we'll investigate how to utilize chuckling to collapse those cash related stresses and transform them into cheerful minutes. Prepare to find out about "Squashing Your Monetary Feelings of trepidation with Parody," where we'll mix humor with monetary insight to make an orchestra of help.

Dread #1: The Feared "B" Word — Planning

Similarly as freestyling on the mic takes practice, so does planning. Rather than seeing it as a requirement, transform planning into an inventive test. Envision you're making a rap section — every dollar has its place, and each cost is a rhyme that adds profundity to your monetary sythesis.

Dread #2: Obligation Beasts Under the Bed

Obligation can feel like that dull rear entryway you'd prefer not to stroll down alone. Yet, prepare to be blown away. You're in good company. Tackle your obligation fears with a comedic wind — envision those Mastercard bills doing the Cha Slide out the entryway as you overcome every one.

Dread #3: The Retirement Void

Retirement arranging could seem like gazing into the void, however consider it outlining your awe-inspiring rap venture. Every venture is a section, and your monetary development is your melodious movement. Furthermore, envision resigning to an existence of spitting shrewdness while tasting a pleasant cold refreshment on a tropical ocean side.

Dread #4: Market Anarchy and Contributing Free for all

The financial exchange can be all around as capricious as an unforeseen rhyme. Embrace the tumult by contrasting it with a free-form rap fight. Once in a while the words simply stream, and different times, it's somewhat of a melodious wreck. Keep your ventures enhanced, and recollect, even the best rap tracks have their highs and lows.

Dread #5: Cash Talks in Connections

Examining funds with an accomplice can be more unnerving than acting before a live crowd. Move toward it like a parody routine — share your cash stories, your monetary goofs, and perhaps toss in some planning jokes to loosen things up. Giggling can facilitate the pressure and help you both get on a similar monetary page.

Dread #6: The Unanticipated Monetary Curves

Similarly as you adjust your sections to various beats, be prepared to adjust to life's monetary curves. Consider these astonishments surprising elements in your rap track. Keep a just-in-case account on backup, and you'll be prepared to drop a few unforeseen monetary sections.

Dread #7: Anxiety toward Passing up a great opportunity (FOMO)

FOMO can prompt incautious spending, such as dropping money on a beat that is not exactly your style. Battle this trepidation by adopting a comedic strategy — envision yourself as an insightful rap pundit, just putting resources into what genuinely resounds with your monetary stream.

Keep in mind: Chuckling as Your Monetary Companion

Similarly as you inject your music with humor, imbue your monetary excursion with giggling. Use parody to vanquish your feelings of dread, transforming nervousness into entertainment. By mixing monetary insight with your interesting funny bone, you're creating a track that is both monetarily keen and extraordinarily engaging.

So, Yo, consider confronting your monetary feelings of trepidation like venturing onto a phase with your mic close by. You have the ability to cut down the house with your comedic take on these concerns. Keep the giggling streaming, and you'll find that those fears transform into zingers in the terrific story of your monetary excursion.

SECTION 9: LOVE AND CASH — A STAND-UP SENTIMENT

Aye yo, G, we should discuss the powerful team of adoration and cash — a couple that is essentially as captivating as a coordinated effort between two specialists. In this part, we're investigating "Love and Cash — A Stand-Up Sentiment," where we'll dive into the entwining dance of connections and funds while imbuing it with your unmistakable humor. Prepare to investigate how love and cash can blend like the ideal rap two part harmony.

Act 1: The Meet-Charming — When Cash Meets Sentiment

Similarly as a tune begins with a fascinating introduction, so does your romantic tale. At the point when cash meets sentiment, it resembles two classes meeting up for a novel cooperation. Examining cash matters right off the bat resembles dropping the beat — an establishment for the fate of your monetary congruity.

Act 2: Planning collectively — Making a Hit Record

Similarly as your music works together various components, so does a relationship. Make a financial plan together, dealing with it like co-setting up a hit account. Each cost is a verse, and every pay source is a congruity. Along these lines, you're creating a monetary tune that resounds with both of you.

Act 3: Monetary Correspondence — The Rap Clashes of Connections

Openness is absolutely vital in the two connections and the music business. With regards to cash, have those rap fight style conversations — open, fair, and with shared regard. Stay away from stowed away charges and shocks, dealing with monetary conversations like uncovering your most true verses.

Act 4: Shared services versus Solo Demonstrations — Tracking down Your Section

Shared services are like coordinated efforts, consolidating assets for a greater effect. Yet, similarly as you keep up with your performance profession, individual records can give a feeling of independence. Balance is the cadence here — finding what turns out best for your organization's one of a kind beat.

Act 5: Objectives and Dreams — A definitive Coordinated effort

Similarly as you work together with individual specialists, team up on your monetary objectives. Dream together, plan together, and pursue those objectives like you're composing the refrains to a graph besting hit. Your association turns into a definitive cooperation, and your monetary achievement is your common melody.

Act 6: Overseeing Clashes — From Breakdowns to Breakbeats

Clashes resemble breakdowns in your rap tracks — they're unavoidable. Yet, similarly as you imbue those breakdowns with strong breakbeats, implant your monetary struggles with understanding and split the difference. Transform conflicts into open doors for development, very much like you would with an inventive riff.

Act 7: Keeping the Satire Alive — Monetary Funnies

Your relationship and monetary excursion resemble a stand-up parody show — loaded with comical minutes. Share monetary funnies, make inside kids about planning accidents, and find humor in those cash related stumbles. Chuckling keeps the sentiment new and the monetary excursion engaging.

Keep in mind: Love and Cash, a Two part harmony for the Ages

Similarly as your rap sections have profundity and layers, so does your relationship with cash. Love and cash, similar to a hit two part harmony, have their highs and lows. Embrace the coordinated effort, impart transparently, and keep the humor streaming. By implanting your romantic tale with monetary insight and a hint of parody, you're making a two part harmony for the ages.

In this way, consider your relationship's monetary excursion like making a significant tune. Every section is a note, every discussion a verse, and your organization a congruity that resounds through time. By exploring affection and cash with the expertise of a carefully prepared lyricist, you're making a stand-up sentiment that is essentially as spellbinding as your best tracks.

CHAPTER 10: LAUGHING ALL THE WAY TO THE BANK

Hey there, It's the ideal opportunity for the fantastic finale of your monetary excursion — the second when all your diligent effort, monetary insight, and humor meet up in an ensemble of progress. Prepare to find out about "Snickering The entire way to the Bank," where we'll praise the triumphs, of all shapes and sizes, that you've accomplished on this monetary experience.

Section 1: From Humble Starting points to Monetary Strut

Similarly as your rap process began with little gigs and developed into sold-out shows, your monetary excursion started with unobtrusive advances. Be that as it may, presently, you're swaggering down the road with the strut of a rap symbol. Your monetary certainty sparkles as brilliantly as your expressive ability.

Section 2: Vanquishing Obligation Like a Rhyme Champion

Recall when obligation felt like a tangled section? You dealt with it directly, handled it sincerely, and transformed those monetary rhymes into a diagram beating hit. Every obligation installment resembled dropping a faultless stanza — perfect, strong, and effective.

Stanza 3: Ventures that Resound with Flourishing

Your venture portfolio resembles an assortment of your most prominent hits — every one resounding with the potential for flourishing. Similarly as you cautiously make your rap refrains, you've cautiously organized your speculations, expanding your monetary tune for an agreeable song of development.

Stanza 4: Retirement, Not Retirement

You may be resigning from your normal everyday employment, except you're not resigning from life. Retirement for you is like changing to your performance vocation — it's an opportunity to investigate new skylines, seek after interests, and keep dropping insight while making every second count.

Stanza 5: Love and Chuckling as Your Monetary Song of praise

Your romantic tale, entwined with monetary humor, resembles a hit hymn that plays behind the scenes of your life. You've explored the ups and downs with chuckling and understanding, making a tune of organization that is pretty much as gorgeous as your most sincere refrains.

Refrain 6: Sharing the Insight, Spreading the Giggling

Similarly as you share your music with the world, share your monetary insight and humor as well. Your process can rouse others to explore their own monetary rap fights cheerfully. Instructing them that cash matters can be drawn nearer with a light heart while as yet being viewed in a serious way.

Chorale: Snickering The entire way to the Bank

Also, presently, you are right here, chuckling the whole way to the bank — allegorically and in a real sense. Your monetary excursion, loaded up with promising and less promising times, wins and afflictions, has driven you to this triumphant melody. You've transformed your monetary dreams into the real world, and the giggling en route has made the excursion even more paramount.

Keep in mind: Your Monetary Heritage

Similarly as your music leaves a heritage, so does your monetary excursion. By imbuing it with humor, insight, and your novel style, you've made an inheritance that will reverberate through time. You've changed monetary difficulties into wins, and your story is a motivation to others setting out on their own monetary experiences.

So, consider this section the awe-inspiring finale of a collection — the crescendo that leaves the crowd applauding more. By snickering the entire way to the bank, you've shown that monetary achievement isn't just about the objective; it's about the excursion, the examples, and the giggling that go with you en route